To Jeff,

Thank you so much for helping me — I know I'm asking a lot on your busy schedule, but I trust you can grasp the testimony of this man and do him justice — I'm looking forward to it —

As always,
Theda

WRITING
BETWEEN THE LINES

WRITING
BETWEEN THE LINES

*A Selection of Poetry
Inspired By Notations in
Alexander Neibaur's Journal
from 1841 until 1862*

Theda Lucille Bassett

ISBN# 0-9661741-0-0

Opinions and information given herein are based on the author's experience and on research believed to be accurate and reliable but not infallible.

Copyright 1997 by Theda Lucille Bassett

All rights reserved, including the right to reproduce this book or portions thereof in any form without prior written permission of Theda Lucille Bassett.

Book design and illustration: Cole & Company, Boise, Idaho.

Printed in the United States of America by Publishers Press
1900 West 2300 South, Salt Lake City, Utah 84119-2014

*Dedicated lovingly to all grandchildren of
Ellen Breakell and Alexander Neibaur
including my sixteen grandchildren*

Alexander and Ellen Neibaur

Comments

In this book of verse, based on her grandfather's journal, Theda Bassett uses her passion for the past, her scholarship, and her skills as a poet, to bring us a fully imagined account of the trials and triumphs of her pioneer ancestors. "Writing Between the Lines" was clearly a labor of love for Ms. Bassett, and in her devotion to family and to her writing, she is an example to us all.

Guy Lebeda, Literature Coordinator
Utah Arts Council, Salt Lake City, Utah

Theda Bassett has given us an epic collection of courage, devotion, and faith. These poems trace the journey of a man and a woman who are undaunted by sorrow and hardship. This poet's work is painstaking and intuitive. The reader will experience the heartache and the triumph of this courageous family who cross the ocean and the bigger part of a continent for their posterity and God.

Elaine Ipson, Past President
Utah State Poetry Society, Stansbury Park, Utah

Contents

Writing Between the Lines

Writing Between the Lines	16

Opposition in All Things

Rhine Fortress on a Hill	18
First Waterloo	19
Opposition in All Things	20
Capturing a Dream in Preston, England 1837	21
Immersed in His Ways	22
Emigration	23
The Longton Cemetery	24
If Oceans Divide us	25
What Will the Ship Be Like?	26
Visiting Mr. Hauk in Liverpool	27
Ship's Steerage	29
Waiting Aboard the *Sheffield*	30

Passage to America

New Passenger on Board the *Sheffield*	32
Hurricane	33
Flogging the Cook	35
Assisting the Steward	36
Flag Flying at Half Staff	37
Jonah Aboard	38
Becalmed at Sea	39
The Brandy Cask	41
Sailing the Gulf of Mexico	42
Crossing the Bar to New Orleans	43
Sailing the Mississippi River	44
New Orleans	45
Mississippi River Snag	46
Memphis Microburst	47
From the Rapids of the Mississippi River at Keokuk	49

In Nauvoo the Beautiful

Getting Land in Nauvoo	51
In Gratitude for Solid Land	52
No Wonder God Said It Was Good	53
Muster on the Fourth of July 1841	54
Alexander Neibaur Surgeon Dentist	55
Visit from Chief Keokuk	56
Death to the Expositor Press	57
Lamentation (written by Alexander Neibaur)	58
Battle of Nauvoo	60
Laying the Nauvoo Temple Capstone	62
Down by the River's Verdant Side	63
Come, Thou Glorious Day of Promise	64

On to Zion

Dentistry in Farmington, Iowa	66
Delivery at Winter Quarters	68
A False Start	69
Lure of Gooseberry Pie	70
Prairie Music	71
Buffalo on the Prairie	72

In the Great Salt Lake Valley

Winter 1848	74
And God Set Rainbows in the Heavens	76
Letters From Silicia	78
Sharing with Strangers	79
Shabbot Text	80
Like the Seagulls	82
Brighton Camp, Cottonwood Canyon, July 24, 1857	83
Torches for the City	84

Contemplations

Father Was It Worth It All?	86
Ethereal Pressure	87
Next Year in Jerusalem	88
Dedication: Orson Hyde Park, Jerusalem, Israel	89
Walk in the Women's Center Garden, Nauvoo	90
Continuum of Green	91
In Their Shadow	92

Preface

Alexander Neibaur was born in 1809 in the Ehrenbreitstein fortress on the French/German border. His Jewish father was surgeon for Napoleon Bonaparte. In his youth, Alexander studied to become a rabbi, but in 1823, went to Berlin to learn dentistry. After graduation in 1826, he practiced on the European continent before moving to Preston, England, to hang his shingle there.

It was here he met Ellen Breakell, an "estimable woman." Ellen was born in Longton, a few miles from Preston. Her family moved to Preston when she was about eleven. Ellen and Alexander married in Chorley in 1834. They were rearing a family when Elders from the Church of Jesus Christ of Latter-day Saints preached in Preston in 1837.

Alexander was immediately convinced, but Ellen struggled until she had her own vision of the truth. They were baptized April 9, 1838, in the River Ribble near their home in Old Cock Yard. Preparations to come to America began soon afterward.

At the beginning of that trip in February 1841 Alexander started a journal which contains many interesting incidents on the 52-day ocean voyage, the three other vessels that carried them up the Mississippi River to Nauvoo, events in Nauvoo, their trek to the Salt Lake Valley, and his first two decades in the valley.

The Neibaurs arrived in Nauvoo at the height of community and mob animosity toward the Mormons. Within a month after his arrival, Alexander not only purchased land, but also added a baby girl to his family and moved into his house. He also joined and trained with the Nauvoo Legion, often tutored the Prophet Joseph Smith in German and Hebrew prior to the Prophet's assassination.

Dr. Neibaur advertised his dentistry practice in the Nauvoo newspaper, <u>The Times and Seasons</u>. His office was in Brigham Young's home. He fought in the Battle of Nauvoo in 1846, left his loved city in September that year with newborn Leah less than a month old. They wintered in Iowa before going to Winter Quarters. At the time of his departure for the valley, his family consisted of seven children, ranging in age from Joseph William 13, to Leah who was 21 months old. They came west with Brigham Young's second company, arriving in the valley September 24, 1848.

Fourteen children were born into the Neibaur family. Their third child, a son Isaac, died in England. The fourth child was also named Isaac, but the first was referred to after his death as Isaac Peretz Samuel. Their eighth child, Rachel, was stillborn in Winter Quarters. Their twelfth child, Mary Esther, lived less than a month in December 1852. Four sons and seven daughters married and continued adding to their parents' posterity which now numbers in the thousands.

Ellen died on 15 December 1870; Alexander lived 13 more years and died 15 December 1883. Both are buried in Salt Lake City cemetery.

Drawings by Reed McGregor

In Appreciation

I am deeply indebted to Alexander Neibaur for keeping a journal with as many details as he did and to both him and his wife for their devotion and dedication, their perseverance during that difficult voyage, their years in Nauvoo, the rigors on the trek west, and their early years in the Salt Lake Valley.

In making a typewritten copy of that journal from his handwritten journal, which is preserved in the Historical Department of the Church of Jesus Christ of Latter-Day Saints, I was filled with questions I could not answer. I wanted to know more details about events where Alexander gave only sketchy notes. I drew time lines to help me understand their ages and those of their children at certain points in their lives. This helped me understand Ellen's reluctance to be baptized, for instance, realizing that in the 1830's a woman with child remained "confined" and would hesitate to go out in public, especially to be immersed in a river.

I acknowledge that in writing poetry in either Alexander's or Ellen's voice, my imagination conjured up details to make the poem work. I caution readers, therefore, to accept as fact only the details from Alexander's journal, but ask you to keep an open mind to the idea that perhaps these grandparents experienced similar feelings to what the poems convey. I do not intend to assume all details are fact, but strived to be as factual as research allowed.

I deliberately did not attempt to write Alexander's feelings about the death of Joseph and Hyrum Smith since he wrote it himself so eloquently, but have included it, his personal testimony, and two of his hymns, all of which enhances this compilation. It humbles me to add my works to his. I hope when I meet them, they will be pleased with my interpretation of their feelings.

I appreciate friends and relatives who encouraged me to keep on with this project, who kept asking for their own copies because they liked what I was doing.

Reed McGregor graciously agreed to permit me to again use his drawings of Alexander and Ellen. I thank him for that.

I am grateful to W. Roger Cole who agreed to do the artwork for this publication on short notice. His knowledge and skills add a dimension I could not achieve alone.

Acknowledgements

Next Year in Jerusalem, published in Bountiful Centennial Collection, 1992, in Zarahemla, 1991

Prairie Music, Second Place Arizona State Poetry Society, published in The Sandcutters, 1993

Jonah Aboard, First Place, Utah State Poetry Society, published in Poetry Panorama, May 1995

Assisting the Steward, published in Neibaur Neighbor newsletter, April 1997

Writing Between the Lines, First Place, League of Mobile Poets, 1997

Dedication: Orson Hyde Park Memorial Gardens, Jerusalem, First Place, California State Poetry Society, 1994, various other honors

Hurricane, Third Place, Utah State Poetry Society, 1997

Winter 1848, Honorable Mention, League of Utah Writers, 1997, Special Recognition, Utah State Poetry Society, 1996

The following are works by Dr. Alexander Neibaur:

ALEXANDER NEIBAUR, SURGEON DENTIST, advertisement in Nauvoo, Illinois Times and Seasons, August 2, 1841

Lamentation, written and published in Nauvoo Times and Seasons in 1844

Down by the River's Verdant Side and *Come, Thou Glorious Day of Promise*, hymns with lyrics by Alexander Neibaur, used courtesy of Church of Jesus Christ of Latter-Day Saints Hymns

Father, Was It Worth It All? Dr. Neibaur's response to his son's question near the end of his life

Writing Between The Lines

I do not pen these lines but for the Gratification of my Posterity...
                          Alexander Neibaur 1869

Writing Between the Lines

Dedicated to Alexander and Ellen Neibaur

I read and re-read the lines you wrote
one hundred fifty years ago,
try to feel what you felt, let your words
transport me back to your 1840's world,
imagine you both young and vigorous.
Through your written words,
I glimpse your ache,
feel the pitch and roll of hurricanes.
I smell the powder fumes
of cannon blast when mobs attack.
I've never lost a child.

Other printed histories speak
about Nauvoo's glory and her doom,
how her people walked down
the Trail of Tears--no looking back.
I've never felt the wrath of angry mobs
and only once have I been forced from home.
I can only vaguely comprehend the dust,
the rain, the calluses endured on your western trek.

When I read between the lines,
I grasp the essence of your dreams,
visualize your realities.
Your penned testimony links me
through you to Elohim.
It is good to know the glory of your days
with the prophet in Nauvoo,
your grief at his martyrdom.
I cherish your persistent spirit
that kept you on Zion's trail.

Because your written words are few,
I search for clues to know those unwritten.
I seek to know more than is revealed.
I keep following your path,
your testimony burning vividly.

Opposition In All Things

For it must needs be, that there is an opposition in all things.

2 Nephi 2:11

Rhine Fortress on a Hill

(Ehrenbreitstein, early 1800's)

Sunup splashes leaf patterns
on the fort, spatters them into my room.
As I poke my head out into misty air,
sunshine raises steam, melts mist away.
Mourning doves coo in nearby birches
whose long shadows stretch across grass.
I want to chase them, watch them shorten
through the day, lengthen when the sun lowers,
reflect on waters where Rhine and Mozelle mix.

Becoming a rabbi requires study every day.
Some mornings the sun cannot penetrate
the mist till long after school begins.
Samuel was young like me when God called him.
I push myself to memorize, read the Torah,
grasp meaning from ancient prophets
who spoke with God.
I answer, Lord, here am I.

School ends, shadows stretch long.
I take my lessons to the fort's west side.
Batteries of Frenchmen guard battlements;
huge cannons pose in readiness.
Soldiers wave me past to enjoy the tinted glow.
The Rhine appears like a rope of molten gold
pouring toward the sea.
Ships and barges plow honeyed curls,
push black dots of swimming ducks to the edge,
leave a rolling trail in their wake.

What a magnificent place to study the Torah!

First Waterloo

I peek through my bedroom door at uniformed men,
strain to hear Father's words with the Emperor Napoleon.
Father sutured wounds, bandaged Napoleon and his men
for years until Father's retirement.
The Emporer calls me by name, ruffles my hair
before I'm sent away. Their tones are private, low.
The Emperor can demand whatever he requires.
What does he ask tonight?

I see Father shake his head.
Napoleon's arms and voice implore.
Father says, *Thank you, no.*
Napoleon stands, *I wish you would reconsider.*
Your language fluency could aid my cause.

Curiosity bites me even more.
Mother peppers questions
as Napoleon's carriage rumbles away.
Their voices are subdued.
I hear Father talk of becoming a spy.

Mother collapses into a chair;
Father strokes her shoulder, comforts,
The risk is far too great.
My growing family needs me.
I've been away too much.

But could he not require it of you? Mother asks.

He could, Father straightens as he speaks,
but he respects the reasons for my choice.

I lie awake, wonder what a spy does,
how being one would aid Napoleon's cause,
why that word makes Mother faint,
how one achieves that respect
which denies the Emperor's request,
yet does not jail Father for saying *No.*

Opposition in All Things

Since Bar Mitzvah my mind churns opposing thoughts.
Father, a skilled surgeon, tells me of France's strides
in dentistry, explains the need for skilled men in that field.

> As a rabbi I would serve my fellowman,
> relieve spiritual pain, perform marriages
> beneath the canopy, teach secular things,
> chant funeral prayers.

A dentist also serves,
relieves the patient's pain.
I am old enough to choose.
Father encourages me and says,
"*Go with Elohim.*"

> After schooling in Berlin, I find myself
> in Preston, England, to work,
> following Elohim like Father said.

I'm drawn to an estimable English maid
who clings to Church of England ways,
communicates freely her opposing views.
I study more, ask Elohim, contemplate.

> I seem compelled to question, to ponder,
> to learn with her, and from her.
> Opposition – her Christianity,
> my long-held traditions as a Jew.

One even deeper opposition – Father.
He gladly sent me to learn dentistry.
He would deny that Jesus Christ
could be our looked-for Messiah.

> In solitude, I talk with Elohim.
> He fills my heart with peace of green landscapes,
> tells me she'll marry me, but not beneath a rabbi's canopy.

Capturing a Dream in Preston, England 1837

In early morning light, Ellen sweeps her stoop.
*"Have you heard about the preachers
who are new in town?"* her neighbor asks.
"They claim they have a Bible, something new."
Ellen lets the news go by.

Her husband steps outside, and asks,
"A Bible? Did I hear you say?"
He demands, *"Where can I find these men?"*

Ellen remembers the nightly dreams he's shared with her,
his deep concerns about what they mean.
She's not surprised when, hat in hand,
he comes and kisses her good-bye.

The Cock Pit Pub is just through the alleyway.
When he returns, his features glow
but not from downing spirits of the Pub
where these men preach. He shows his wife
the *Book*, proclaimed to be accompaniment
to the Bible they use.

For three days, this scriptorian is engrossed
in history contained between the *Book's* fresh leathered frame.
He hungers for neither food nor drink.
The children's noisy play does not disturb
his study of this work. He feasts on Isaiah's words,
as well as prophets new to him.
He acts enchanted by phrases he knows,
by promises of God to Israel's hosts,
especially to his Judah line.
He wears the glow of Moses after Mount Sinai.

Immersed in His Ways

Baptism, baptism, Ellen thinks.
Alexander constantly asks,
but I'm not ready.
I'm heavy with his child.
What if they couldn't pull
      me up
from the River Ribble's murk?
Maybe next spring
when I'm less cumbersome.

Baptism. What's wrong
with Church of England ways?
Immersion, Alexander says.
I know how he sacrificed,
put his Jewish life aside, alienated
family he still loves, to recognize
the Messiah is Jesus Christ.

The River Ribble runs
swift and deep, floods
with incoming tides.
I've watched others wade in,
be laid down, rejoice when lifted out.

This April day the roily Ribble waters
are Priesthood-blessed. They feel
like melted snow, cause me to catch my breath
as I wade beyond my knees, up to my waist.
Brother Russell's arm raises to the square.
I snatch one long breath during his short prayer.
I am engulfed. I return Alexander's approving smile
when I am lifted up. He wraps me in a blanket,
gives me a squeeze,
          turns, wades in.

Emigration

My parents moved from Longton
to Preston when I was young.
Those towns are only miles,
not oceans, apart.
Now he wants to emigrate,
sail to America to meet this prophet
God raised up.
I must leave family and friends behind,
leave our son's grave unattended here.

Perhaps I should rejoice.
In Preston I met this Jew,
a spiritual man, well-read,
willing to change once he is convinced.

My family would write to me.
As a Christian, his family considers him dead.
He never complains,
writes them anyway.
He earns our keep through dentistry.

Our children are hearty enough to make the trip.
Still, I cannot say I want to go.
He asks hard things,   and yet,
he asks no more of me
than he will have to give.

The Longton Cemetery

Before departing England,
I take Joseph and Margaret with me
to visit the town where I was born.
With their small hands in mine,
we walk around the house.
I tell them, *My family moved
before I was twelve.
I made new friends, adjusted.*
(This for myself more than for them).
We sit inside the chapel
where I was christened and first baptized.

Still hand in hand, we amble
through tall grasses
growing gangly
near gray tombstones.
I tell them these are family names,
other grandparents, etched here in black.
Our fingers touch indentations
of their kin's names.
We place fresh flowers near the stones.

Tears fall on moss-covered ancestral stones.
Small consoling hugs ease my constricting pain.
I have not the heart to tell them
that, in America, we'll be too far away
to put fresh flowers on new mounds
when the grandparents they know in England die.

If Oceans Divide Us

Isaac, my son, this stone
marking your resting place
is as heavy and cold as my heart.
I still dream of those last days,
rocking your frail body, trying
to find nourishment for you.
Neither doctors, love, nor tears
could halt your decline.

England's winter fog settled
across your brown eyes,
once full of wonder,
mischievousness.
I couldn't distill the overcast.
You now smile at God,
leaving me longing.

The brother God sent us
after He called you home
grows stronger every day.
We named him Isaac to honor you.
He does not replace you in my heart,
nothing can do that. Caring for him
eases my pain in losing you.

Your father says we're going to America.
That same fog envelops my heart.
I dread leaving you here.
Remember, though oceans divide us,
the stone of my sorrow remains at your head.
The sunshine of your brief life ever lifts me,
will transport me
across oceans to be with you.

What Will the Ship Be Like?

Feb 5th 1841 left Preston Lancashire England in Company my wife 3 children & a Number of others for Liverpool to embark on board the Ship the <u>Sheffield</u> bnd for New Orleans

My children question me about our trip,
are eager to embark, wonder a lot.
The answers I am unprepared to give.
I cannot let them know I am distraught.

We are not like Christopher Columbus
sailing for an uncharted, unknown shore.
The captain who commands this ship is skilled,
has sailed the Atlantic many times before.

With charts and precise compasses, he knows
wind currents, how to manage in rough seas.
His crew is trained to handle sails in wind
and how to deal with every kind of breeze.

We will make friends with other passengers;
this is the first I've left our English isle
so cannot say for sure how it will be,
but we will be together all the while.

Our days aboard the ship may seem quite long;
it's hard to find something I can compare.
We must not dwell on other wrecks at sea.
We place our trust in God's protecting care.

Visiting Mr. Hauk in Liverpool

Feb 6th ...I went to see a frnd of mine Mr Hauk He was very glad to see me and particular so that I made up my mind to emigrate He gave me a present for my wife a Boa a muff for my daughter and a pair of fur Gloves for myself wisht me a safe arrival that the Lord might prosper me...

Alexander secures a scarf around Isaac's head,
lifts him to his shoulders for the winding walk
up to Liverpool. Margaret and Joseph bound ahead
in barely warm February sun.

At Mr. Hauk's leather goods store, a bell announces customers.
Leather permeates the air; bags hang on pegs,
line shelves. Furs are encased in glass or hang on racks.

"Alexander Neibaur, how nice to see you."
The men shake hands, renew acquaintances.
"I'd like you to meet my family." Alexander
places Isaac on a vacant stool, motions
his children near, speaks their names.
Hauk asks, "What brings you to Liverpool?"

"We sail tomorrow to America aboard the Sheffield."
"I know it," says Hauk, "It's good. Why so far?"
Alexander watches to see how his words fall.
"I joined the Mormons, and I can get land."
No condescension there. Hauk says, "That's good."
He turns to Ellen, "A long trip for a small family.
Are you concerned?" Ellen pulls on her reserves,
"We will survive."
Margaret clings to her; Ellen snuggles her close.

Hauk notes Margaret's timidity, turns to Joseph,
"Quite an adventure for a boy. How old are you?"
Joseph speaks up, "Seven, sir."
"Yes, quite grown up. You'll be a help. Ever been at sea?"

Joseph tucks his head, modestly answers, "No."
"That's all right, few who sail these days have been."

While the men visit, Ellen hovers near. Her children look
through glass at encased goods until Hauk speaks,
"I have a gift for you."

He pulls a length of mink from the glass case,
hands it to Ellen. *"This boa will ward off winter cold,
both here and in America."* He hands Alexander gloves.
"These are fur-lined to warm your hands," he says.
Alexander smiles, says thanks.

Hauk takes a rabbit fur muff from a peg,
entreats Margaret to reach out her hand. She checks
with Mother to be sure, reaches shyly to accept.
She cannot hide her beaming face once the muff is in her arms.
Ellen puts the strap around her daughter's neck;
Margaret stuffs her hands inside.
Hauk smiles approval at her soft *"Thank you."*

He looks at Joseph, scratches his head.
"I have just the thing for you, my lad."
He takes matching mittens and scarf from his display,
wraps the scarf around Joseph's neck, holds one mitten
while the boy dons the first.
"We can't forget the baby." Hauk selects
a folded blanket from the shelf.

The family thank their generous host,
promise to send an address in America.
The children walk outside. Father says,
*"How kind of Mr. Hauk.
We all wear something new
to bless our journey to this new land, America."*

Ship's Steerage

Feb 5th 1841...A number of us went to the Hargreaves Railway Office for our luggage got this on board got something from the cook shop for our families as it was very cold went to bed at dark.

The huge room below the *Sheffield's* deck fills
with travelers, confusion.
Slivered bare boards of bunk beds
line exterior walls, look uninviting, hard.
Nothing is assigned; no one in charge.

Alexander and I select a corner pair of bunks for privacy.
We'll put Joseph and Isaac at one end, Margaret
opposite. We'll snuggle close below.
The narrow bunks are barely wide enough for one.
My protruding stomach needs extra room.

I look at long benches stretched the length
of tables in the room, all securely nailed.
I see solitude depart as more
of two hundred thirty fellow travelers board.

Alexander returns from Hargreaves Railway
with our trunk. I line hard wood with quilts.
He brings us food from the cook's shop.
The night is bitter cold; robbers abound outside.
We'll eat inside and go to bed.

Our family kneels. *"Dear God, we thank Thee
for our safe trip. Please protect us as we sail to America."*
I touch my bulging stomach, in silence
add, *"And please, God, give me strength
to endure a month of this togetherness."*

Waiting Aboard the *Sheffield*

Febr 6th...toward dark Elders Young Tailor Richards which 3 gentlemen had the superintendency of the storing for the Company arrived as Elder Hyram Clark the President for the Voyage After the emigrants were called to order by B Young and silence being attained the Company was ordered to be on board by 8 o'clock on Sunday mourning and all those that had not paid their full passage or deposited 2£. towards their provision would be put ashore luggage & all those that had not done so was ordered to go Imidiately to 72 Borlington St. There were several that were compelt to borrow. Proctor was forcet to pawn his clothes

It's hard to think within this bedlam of anxiety.
Ellen's children play around tied-down trunks.
She must speak above the noise to get them to respond.

Brigham Young and his two counselors come aboard.
"*Brothers and Sisters,*" he calls out. "*Quiet, please.*"
Gradually the talking diminishes.
"*This is Elder Hyrum Clark. He will be in charge
when your company sails tomorrow.
If you go ashore, be back aboard by eight.*"
He pauses, glances at this gathering.
"*Those who have not paid their full passage
plus two pounds for provisions on the ship,
do it today.*" He shakes his head,
"*Those not paid will be put ashore, luggage and all.*"

Muffled grumblings grow.
Ellen barely hears Brother Brigham say,
"*Have a safe voyage. God be with you.*"

That night Alexander whispers names
of families forced to borrow to stay aboard.
"*Proctor pawned his clothes to pay passage for his family.*"
Ellen kisses Alexander's cheek,
caresses features she has grown to love,
sees him tuck covers about the children's chins.
She sighs, relieved their passages are paid.

Passage To America

Feb 5th 1841 left Preston Lancashire England in company my wife 3 children...to embark on board the ship the <u>Sheffield</u> bnd for New Orleans...

Alexander Neibaur

New Passenger on Board the *Sheffield*

February 11, 1841 Some passengers Received ahead [aboard] towards evening one of the passengers from Preston a Woman dangerous ill died about 12 1/2 o.

A Preston lady came on board quite ill.
The men made space; they carried her along.
She wanted Zion, but had lost her will

to stay alive. She quickly went downhill.
The sisters prayed with her all morning long.
A Preston lady came on board quite ill.

She rallied, seemed imbued with strength until
some thought she would improve, but they were wrong.
She wanted Zion, but had lost her will

to fight. She took a turn, by noon was chill.
She gave up Zion though she seemed headstrong.
This Preston lady came on board quite ill,

became the *Sheffield's* first to lie death-still.
Some gawking sailors joined the curious throng.
She wanted Zion, but had lost her will.

One member sewed her in a sheet, with skill;
the Captain said, *"Heav'n's where you belong."*
A Preston lady came on board quite ill.
She wanted Zion, but had lost her will.

Hurricane

Feb. 11, 1841 Towards 6 o'clock wind ahead blows fresh increases to a hurricane...
Elder H: Clark just making some Remarks on the Burial of our Beloved Sister the Ship heaving most trementously tubbs roling about Pans Kettles and cans all in a uproar woman shrieking children crying all hastning to the Betts wind contin all night Right ahead very Strong

I am relieved when Alexander comes below at dusk.
For hours the ship has tipped port side,
                              rocked   back.
Hurricane force winds rile these Atlantic seas,
drop the ship into gigantic swells,
              spew sheets of spray across the decks.
He watched sailors lash down sails
              so winds would not rip them apart.

Pots and pans clang.
                    Unanchored tubs and barrels
shift.   Even people tilt
who are not holding tight.
              Kerosene lanterns sway,
       cast eerie shadows.
                    We women try not to scream,
know it increases our children's fright.
       We cannot contain our fear
              of each fierce roll.

Alexander talks in quiet tones
to our small ones,   tucks them in,
keeps a pan nearby and holds their heads.
       I cannot do a thing.
My stomach rumbles like this gnarly sea.
       I retch and sweat,   grow weak.
My body groans like the creaking
of the vessel's rubbing wood,
              twisted and stressed by a churning sea.

33

The sour steerage stench
                and constant
      pitch and roll
trigger continual volleys of upheaval,
       smelled and heard
from every side,
dimmed only by the chaos of clanging pots,
               s l i d i n g trunks.
  Nourishment is sparse for my kicking child
       rebelling in my womb
             each time I hang my head.

Flogging the Cook

Feb 17, 1841 Cook neglecting his duty got flockt 24 lashes having to much liquor given him by the Company...

Captain Porter insists all male passengers observe
on deck the discipline their generosity caused.
"I don't care," he said in a matter-of-fact way,
"which man of you is at fault.
Someone gave too much brandy to my cook.
Now he must pay for his neglect."

The cook waits, lashed to the main mast,
his body bare above his waist, brown, glistening,
ripples of his rotund chest stretched taut,
diminished by pull of tied-up arms.

Passengers hug the ship's sides, stacked two
and three deep. They stand away from the mast,
the man. Captain Porter, on the quarter deck, shouts,
"I must remind you, my men have duties at sea."
He surveys these Saints, their eyes down-cast.
"This must not happen again." To his Mate,
commands, *"Begin."*

Men hear the staccato snap of whip,
see the cook wince. Each blow draws blood,
raises welts accompanied by pain.
Men cringe, look beyond the man,
beyond the whip, to horizons,
or to boards coursing the deck.

Each silently counts, 21, 22, 23, 24,
weighs the consequence of this deed.
No one points an accusing finger
nor speaks aloud for hours.

Assisting the Steward

*Mar 3, 1841 fine mourning hot sun Little breeze
Drawing a tooth for the steward Ship in Sight at a
distance*

The steward with a tooth complaint
shows great restraint.
He asks, point-blank,
if I will yank
his tooth. It causes nightly pain.
He does explain
how bothersome
it has become.
The sun blazes with little breeze.
I pull and squeeze,
relieve distress,
apply compress.

Flag Flying at Half Staff

Mar 4 1841 hot Mourning more than any hot Summers day in England Ship in Sight draws near her flag half mast high discernable through the Glass the Captain thinking she is in distress orders the Sails down to wait for her, tacking about. toward 4 o'clock as she came nearer the Capt discovered his Mistake. she being an American having her colour out in honour of the new President General Harrison taking the chair when he discovered his mistake he ordered the Sail up again almost dead calm Quit [quite] calm at night.

As a lad in France, Father's fidelity to Napoleon
insured his position as surgeon in his employ.
Father told me, *"We give respect to Napoleon,
but we serve Jehovah and Elohim."*
Our kin live in Prussian towns,
but Europe's borders shift with wars
like Sahara's sands blown by Mediterranean winds.

I hung my shingle in England's Preston town,
respected her monarch, though my allegiance
will ever be to Jehovah and Elohim.
I speak seven languages; God understands
no matter which I use in prayer.
I'll use English in America, a land free
of emperors and kings, a place where I can purchase land.

How must I change? Though I maintain devotion
to Elohim, how does one merge from German,
French, or Prussian to become American?
I am like that ship whose flag flew low as if distressed.
My heart feels at half mast–for loved ones
who cannot accept Christ as the Messiah,
for ingrained traditions I have put aside,
for newness of life that surges within me
with vibrant hopes in this new land.
Like the flag, I flutter in the winds of uncharted challenges.

Jonah Aboard

Mar 5 1841 ...no wind, dead calm Ship steering S:S:E: Proctors child dies the Captain saying to Br Miles Rumly there must be some unfortunate Jonas on Board as the Ship is so becalmt ... in the course of the day some serious thing took place Elder Clark being charged with behaving himself unseemingly to Sister Marie Hardman & other Females, some hard words passing between the parties. This is the first day that my Wife missed being sea sick...

Last week's Sunday services were long sitting in the sun.
Many sunburned. Today the Captain orders a sail
for shade. Ellen with the children, strolls the deck, enjoys
sunshine's warmth, the ocean, mirror smooth.
      No hint of winds to fill the sails.
She hears sailors grumble at the calm, but she rejoices.
I can eat the soup and, better yet, can keep it down.

She overhears the Captain say, *"Strange, for these seas
to be so still at this latitude.
There must be some unfortunate Jonah aboard."*

Ellen thinks, Come now, Captain, the fourth night out
when that hurricane raged, I, too, wondered if Jonah
were aboard. Certainly not today in this quietude.
      Yet, perhaps you're right.
Proctor's child was buried yesterday at sea.
Now Elder Clark's accused of behaving himself
unseemingly toward Sister Marie.

The service begins, ends Ellen's reverie.
Brother Frances sings a hymn, preaches righteousness,
alludes to accusations made against Elder Clark.
"All must confess," he says, *"be reconciled,
before receiving sacrament."*
Elder Clark, choking with tears, begs forgiveness
of all for any offense in either word or deed.

Perhaps now, Captain, winds will resume.

Becalmed at Sea

Mar 17, 1841 Fine Mourning About 8 o clock as the first mate came to the men to give orders about the painting one of the Men Struck at him 3 times. the mate having treadnet the previous Night to Split his Skull for having pullet the Sheet of him and Alice Standing a young Woman from Preston. the Captain came with Handcuffs to Confine the Offender, but some Resisdence being offeret to him he went to the Cabin fetchet a Sword and said he was determinet to Support his Authority and any off the Men Resisding him he would Split them in two if he has Strength in his Arm...he said Passengers the Ship is in a State of Mutiny look out, your wifes & childrens life is in danger...

For three days now the sea lies calm,
not a whisper of wind to fill the sails.
I stroll the deck with my family, glad my wife is well.
Other passengers, recovering from rolling seas, also stir,
stroll in sunshine on the decks.

It seems lack of wind raises tempers like wind-tossed seas.
Sharp tongues lash out like sudden squalls.
Disputes emerge, roll like voluminous waves among us.
In the calm we forget the endured hurricane,
the rings around the moon.
Perhaps we've been at sea too long.

The First Mate orders his painting crew on deck.
Some Saints harass the working seamen,
accuse the Mate of keeping a crew without seamanship.
The Mate ignores their taunts,
remains as calm as these breeze-less days.
One can see his temper heat like windless decks.

An angry seaman lashes out at the Mate.
With each punch, he claims revenge
for threats hurled by the Mate the previous night.
The Mate accepts the blows, stands firm,
retorts, *"I'll split your skull for pulling the sheets
off me and that Preston maid!"*

Captain Porter intervenes, halts the blows,
orders handcuffs. The seaman resists.

"We'll see!" the captain says. He departs,
returns with sword in hand, states,
"I am determined to support my authority.
Any resisters will be split in two
if I have strength in these two arms."

The sailor scurries below, refuses restraints.
Captain Porter looks around at throngs
of Saints strolling on decks, young children at their sides.

He shouts, "I would not hurt the hair of any head
unless I'm forced." He turns and warns,
"This ship's in mutiny. Look out!
Your wives' and children's lives are in jeopardy."

Concerned parents gather children,
file down the passageway to steerage gloom.

Captain Porter calls to the Company's man,
"Please come with me."
Saints see the captain's cabin door close.
When Elder Clark returns, he calls his Saints
to the afterdeck. "Captain Porter needs volunteers
to stand by him in securing the offender. Who will help?"

Richard Whittnall bows, steps forth.
Four other men follow Elder Clark.
Each is issued a fully charged stand of arms.
In single file behind the captain, they march below,
stand nervously in passageways, muskets in readiness.

"This is the Captain. I order you,
as your friend, to deliver yourself up peaceably."

      Silence hangs
as endless as hurricanes and squalls,
as unmoving as sails hanging limp.
Six men sigh to see the sailor emerge.
He's handcuffed, confined to a long boat,
to be trailed behind the ship.

Volunteers return the guns, rejoin the group.
They're greeted, not with cheers of gratitude or praise,
but with fault-finding that they took up arms.

Yes, Captain, we've been at sea too long.

The Brandy Cask

Mar 20 ...in Sight N W 2 ships for Jamaica about 4 1/2 a cry was Raised Ship on fire many of the Passengers and crew hastning about woman coming & Running to the forecastle some crying some Almost fainting. This ship is on fire & some hastning with Buckets and cans of Water...

Fire! Fire! Ship's on fire!

Ellen smells the smoke.
Some women scream, others faint,
act like fumes will overpower them.
Ellen grabs the baby,
helps her toddlers up the passageway
toward the forecastle deck.
Alexander finds his family safe,
joins men grabbing buckets,
cans of water, rushing below.

"*There's no concern,*" states Elder Clark.
"*The fire's out. It was my fault.*"
He's very nonchalant.

Ellen and her children stay on deck
till Alexander returns, curls
them in his arms. "*It's safe now,*"
he says, shaking his head.
"*George Scoles helped put it out.
His face is burnt. I did what I could to help.*"

He smiles, whispers to his wife, "*Elder Clark
drew some spirits from the brandy cask,
then without thinking, struck a match
to see how much was left.*"

Sailing the Gulf of Mexico

22 Mar 1841 Fine Morning Spoke the Julius of Plymouth Am from Rio Janeiro bnd for New Orleans cargo coffee Miles Hodgson's wife delivered of a Boy...

Each day we are encouraged out on deck.
We see plantations on the nearby isles.
Islands near Cuba can be seen for miles;
some on horizons look like tiny specks.
My spouse gets joy from noting passing ships,
where they are from, and also where they're bound.
The size of dolphin caught seem to astound
my dentist spouse. With tenderness he grips
his children's hands, shows them wonders of earth
not seen in Preston streets. I answer calls
to join the sisters who create the walls
of privacy for Sister Hodgson's birth.
    The sea's been home, but we have not been friends.
    I touch my roundness, glad this journey ends.

Crossing the Bar to New Orleans

29 Mar 1841 cool Morning towards 6 o'clock discryt [sic] the Steamer coming out towards 7 another Steamer coming also a pilot belonging to the first Steamer about 8 o'clock steamer [coming] and pilot close too the Pilot came on Board the steamer <u>Tenessy</u> taking in towe Wind right ahead passed the bar about 12 o'clock...

At last! There's New Orleans in view.
Our trunks are packed.
We'll transfer to another ship.
Inspectors allow this ship to pass.
We anchor in the gulf.
A pilot takes the *Sheffield* across the bar.

The steamer *Tennessee* at noon tows us
close in, the pilot unconcerned
about how we dip and roll.
We are reminded again of that hurricane
as the pilot takes the *Sheffield* across the bar.

Provisions are divided among passengers.
Grumbling grows on every side, rises
and falls like last month's ocean swells,
becomes like the surging sea
fighting for supremacy
of ebb and flow
against the mighty Mississippi.
We pilot ourselves across this roily bar.

Sailing The Mississippi River

March 30 1841 fine frosty Morning passet the English-turn many fine plantations Negroes at work about 3 oclock passet the Barraks cast ancor about 4 oclock in the Afternoon as soon as the Ship was fastned Richard Wittnall myself and many more went on shore a Number of men came on board Sevreal of the Passengers made purchases in Provisions at night as there was many Strangers on Board we agreed amongst ourselfs 2 men to Watch at each hatchway for 2 hours in their turn

In early morning aboard the ship *Morovian*,
we start up the Mississippi River in grand style.
River plantations line each bank.
Black workers move like ants on peony leaves,
hover in greening fields in frosty air.
We pass some barracks at three,
anchor at four for wood.
Richard Whitnall and I go for provisions
in the town. Strangers come on board
to sell their wares to those who stay.

So many strangers move about,
we fear they are like ants, ready to converge
on any possessions not put away.
They move among us,
colorful cloths tied round their heads,
ant colonies on crusade.

Like warrior ants protecting our domain,
we volunteer for a two-hour watch at each hatchway.

New Orleans

March 31 1841 fine frosty Morning it was quit [sic] a change having been Melted with heat for the last 4 weeks now many Complaint about colt... in the Afternoon it was Reported the Steward had the Cook taken up to Sell him New Orleans in Luisiana being one of the chief Slave states Mr Clark having been with the Captain to the Costume [custom] house brought Permits to pass us...

All bundle warm who come on deck.
Even when the sun is high, chill breezes blow.
Grumbling is heard on every side.
Some grumble if it's hot,
others if it's cold.

While I clean the teeth of both the Mates,
Elder Clark returns from Customs with permits.
The Company can complete its travels to Nauvoo.
He should be rejoicing, but seems downcast.
He reports the Steward sold the cook
for a slave in New Orleans.

A chill shivers me,
as if an Arctic breeze blew by.
America, land of the free,
except here in Louisiana,
a state allowing slaves.

I sigh,
hope freedom means free for all
in Illinois where we are bound.

Mississippi River Snag

April 8, 1841 Fine Mourning passet several fine plantations wood toward 7 o'clock at evening passengers come Running from the foredeck aloft all were hastening to the top crying the Boat is sinking...

The ship bumps hard,
jars all inside, thumps and stalls
in the Mississippi River
beyond Vicksburg.

"Boat sinking!" passengers yell.
Panic prevails.
Women scream,
children cry,
fearful husbands hurry
from the foredeck aloft.
Seamen draw buckets of water,
prime the pumps.
The Mate, with a kerosene lantern,
goes to the hold,
inspects bulkheads of his ship.
He tells his passengers,
*"The ship has hit a snag,
but no damage is done.
There's no danger."*

Wailing dies.
Muttering passengers descend
to crowded beds.

"Man overboard!"
The Mate holds up his lantern
to find the floundering man.
"Lower a bucket!" the Mate yells.
Harrison hangs on.
Seamen and saints pull him aboard.
Dripping water from pants and sleeves,
he smiles, *"I'm much obliged!"*

Memphis Microburst

April 9, 1841 towards 9 o'clock the Sky began to lower at Midnight it thundered and lightning illuminated the Objects around us for many a Mile...

We join passengers who go ashore in Memphis.
The *Morovian* takes on wood.
The magnolias and flowering trees enchant us.
Our children run free while we watch clouds gather.
By our return, they've obliterated the sun.
At nine o'clock they darken, solidify.

Toward midnight lightning illuminates
the Mississippi River for miles.
It brightens landscapes and towns on either bank.
Claps of thunder blast like cannons,
roar repeatedly with little respite,
shake the ship, rattle the nerves of passengers.

Sparks fly in the steerage. *"Fire! Fire!"*
Women scream; children wail.
Men extinguish flames,
flailing them with coats.
All who tried to sleep, wake,
add their own disorder
to the storm's resounding bedlam.

One lightning bolt blows the cookhouse windows out.
The cook deserts his kitchen home,
scampers to be with companions
on the quarterdeck. Another strike shatters
wheelhouse windows where he ran.
The men, deafened, stunned, have nowhere to run.

"Make for land till daylight!"
The captain, alarmed by this display,
shouts, *"Stop the engines!"*

Anchored at sanctuary of river bank,
crew and passengers watch and pray

while the storm rages. Wary seamen
and weary travelers heed thunder rumbles,
wince as lightning picks scenes to show.

By morning the show moves east.
Survivors view its destructive path,
visible in upturned trees,
houses shaken down,
roofs askew,
walls laid flat.

In awe, groups of Saints point
where wind and rain prevailed.
They speak with gratitude for morning sun.

From the Rapids of the Mississippi River at Keokuk

April 18, 1841 fine Morning no boat began to Rain...a steamboat the <u>Aster</u> came along side she carried us up to Nauvoo the place of our destination all the goods belonging to the Company was here discharged A Number of the Br was ready to Receive us they kindly offeret their houses many slept in a large stone building belonging to one of the Br Myself & Wm Cross with some others Kept up a large fire all night and stayet with our luggage..

The captain ascertains the *Goddess of Liberty*
cannot go further up the Mississippi River from Keokuk.
He'll engage a keel boat to take us to the first steamer
able to carry us to Nauvoo.
All trunks and goods are discharged.
The family ambles around Keokuk,
not venturing far from the docks.

Elder Clark departs immediately for Nauvoo,
arranges for the steamboat *Aster* to take us
to our destination–Nauvoo–a name so long on our lips,
ever distant, a promise unfulfilled.

We disembark,
rejoice to see our trunks discharged.
A sweep of greenery surrounds homes
dotting Nauvoo's landscape. Citizens shake our hands,
welcome us into their homes like long-missed kin.

My pregnant wife and our children go to a home.
William Cross and I join others who keep a vigil
near the docks. A large fire warms us.
Sitting on our trunks, we speculate about the land,
what it will grow, where ours will be along this river,
but most of all, we wonder
how it will be to meet a prophet of the Lord.

In Nauvoo the Beautiful

a Number of the Br was ready to Receive us they kindly offeret their houses...

Alexander Neibaur

Getting Land in Nauvoo

Apr 22 went to see Br Thompson about some land promiset I should have some

Apr 23 Fine day went to the Office of Thompson where some of the Br Kings was to be tried for felony a waggon having been taken from the premises of the Marshal of the City which he had securet from King King was taken in Custody for the same but after being examinet before the Mayor was discharget–Prepared some wood for fencing.

First thing I asked about was land.
"If I had means, [I] could get some..."

Brother Thompson was the man to see.
At Thompson's home, however,
a Brother King was being tried for felony,
his crime, taking a wagon
from the marshal's land.
After much discussion,
the mayor discharged the case.

The following day the militia trained;
I am a new recruit. On the Sabbath,
Mayor Bennett, William Law,
and the Prophet Joseph spoke
till four o'clock, with a request
for Secret Service volunteers.

I've been casting up a train for Brother Joseph.
My first free day, I see Thompson about land.
I acquire a quarter-acre lot,
opposite Mr. Tidwell, the cooper, and
close to Brother Joseph's Mansion House.

Some brethren volunteer to help me build my house.
I tell my wife I'll fence our land,
till and plant a garden for us here.

In Gratitude for Solid Land

May 2 1841 Br Miles Hodgson died... May 22 Wife was brought to Bett of a Girl May 29 moved into my house

Yesterday Sister Hodgson's heart spilled again
with grief over her husband's death.
Her baby's barely three weeks old.
Now her husband's dead.
She feels like a stranger in Nauvoo,
alone, in spite of friends.
I comfort her as best I can.

While labor pains increase in frequency today
for me, I recall her delivery a month ago
in the crowded steerage of the ship.
Blankets were hung for privacy;
women's skirts created walls
to keep out prying eyes,
but offered little to diminish
the agony of birthing pains.

Sister Hodgson helped me through my first month
of constant nausea aboard the ship.
Despite being quite cumbersome,
she brought sustenance for my family
when I could hardly move.
Each night I gave thanks for getting nearer to land
before this child would birth.
              God obliged.

We are all strangers here, living, dying,
working, giving birth in someone else's home,
sharing a sisterhood of strength with God.

My eyes roll as each pain presses,
but it is not the ship being tossed at sea.
It's only me thrashing against the push,
not waves oversplashing the ship.
The beat in my ear drums echoes only my heart,
not the clang of pans and buckets
rattling with every sway of wave.
Within the hour I present my husband
this child, our first born in this new land.

No Wonder God Said It Was Good

I love the smell of newborn flesh,
the velvet texture of baby's skin.
I love how it changes day to day,
like a chameleon reflecting vermillion,
ocher, and delicate cream.
I love to watch the varied movements
in lips and face as muscles
rehearse their supple needs.
I love the different cries that clue
parents to baby's needs, that nuzzling
of flesh when hunger comes.
I marvel how each nail, each lash,
each ear and eye grow perfectly
from two minute particles.
I warm as smiles grow from within,
the gooing that speaks contentment.

The miracle of life stirs deep,
repeats, and God sees it is good.

Muster on the Fourth of July 1841

July 4 1841 Nauvoo, Illinois celebration of American Indep Grand Parade of Nauvoo Legion 4 Comp from Burlington come down on a Steam Boat

Strangers travel great distances, file into Nauvoo
to celebrate America's independence day.
They come in elegant buggies with matching teams.
Some ride on horseback, or plod along
with oxen teams pulling rigs.

I join the Legionnaires regaled in full dress uniform,
our muskets shouldered, swords swinging at our hips,
boots polished to a shine.
Two months ago at Brother Joseph's request,
I volunteered. Since then, we've trained for parade.

At three o'clock the artillery blasts several cannon rounds,
announces the arrival of Lieutenant General Smith.
He inspects his uniformed militia, all standing straight.

My mind retains a childhood memory
of the Emperor Napoleon Bonaparte
riding before his troops, his body straight
astride his prancing horse, his sword hanging from his belt.

The Lieutenant General salutes, signals the band.
Speakers remind us a mere 65 years have passed
since America declared independence,
won it from the Crown. My heart is full.
These three months I've thrived in that freedom.
The fireworks at dusk reflect my gratitude,
exploding from me like the crowd's *oh's* and *ah's*.

Alexander Neibaur, Surgeon Dentist

(Written by Alexander)
August 2, 1841 "<u>Times and Seasons</u>" Nauvoo, Illinois

From Berlin, in Prussia, late of Liverpool
and Preston, England. Most respectfully
announces to the ladies and gentlemen
and the citizens of Nauvoo
as also of Hancock county, in general,
that he has permanently established himself
in the city of Nauvoo, as a dentist,
where he may be consulted daily,
in all branches connected with his profession.

Teeth cleaned, plugged, filed,
and Scurva effectually cured,
children's teeth regulated, natural
or artificial teeth from a single tooth
to a whole set inserted
on the most approved principle.

Mr. N. having had an extensive practice
both on the continent of Europe,
as also in England, for the last 15 years
he hopes to give general satisfaction to all those
who will honor him with their patronage.

Mr. B. Young having known Mr. N. (in England)
has kindly consented to offer me his house to meet
those ladies and gentlemen who wish to consult me.
Hours of attendance from 10 o'clock
in the morning to 6 at evening.

My own residence is opposite Mr. Tidwell,
the cooper, near the water. Ladies and gentlemen
attended at their own residence if requested.
Charges strictly moderate.

Visit From Chief Keokuk

Aug 12, 1841 a tribe of Indians came over the Mississippi with their chief Kiuky at their head they were in their full dress also their Squas They were Received by the Mayor of Nauvoo with a Band of Music the chief officers of the Nauvoo legion in their Uniform and a Number of the Citiecens joining in Procession

"*The Indians will not come ashore unless you bid them yourself,*"
the Prophet's told.   Brother Joseph joins the military band,
the detachment of Invincibles (of which I am a part)
to welcome them ashore.   The ferryman escorts
these tribes of Sac and Fox across the Mississippi River
from Montrose. They come with full headdresses,
feathers flouncing in the wind,
long black braids beneath.
Beads on moccasins and tunics adorn their clothes.

Brother Hyrum introduces the Prophet to Chief Keokuk,
Chiefs Kis-ku-kosh and Appenoose.
Perhaps a hundred other chiefs and braves
and their accompanying squaws march
in procession to the village green.
They sit cross-legged on the grass;
the band and Legion members form an outer ring.

With them in the inner court, the Prophet,
through his interpreter, emphasizes promises
gleaned from Book of Mormon pages,
states these promises extend to Keokuk and all his kin.
He entreats the Chief, "*Cease killing each other now,
stop warring with the other tribes, keep peace with whites.*"

Chief Keokuk tells the Prophet, "*In my tepee, I have book
you gave me many moons ago.*" He adds, "*I look rough,
but I, too, am son of Great Spirit.
I follow good talk you give.*"
After feasting on foods, dainties, and watermelons,
Indians perform ceremonial dances to thank their host.
They dance and drum until the hour grows late.

Death to the Expositor Press

*June 10, 1844 City council order the Expositor Press to be
Destroyet consider it a newsance*

My company of the Nauvoo Legion is ordered
in readiness to assist
in the destruction of the Expositor Press.
The City Council voted their libelous works
to be a nuisance and a threat
to the Charter of Nauvoo.

The city marshal demands the keys
to the building that houses the press.
Mr. Higbee denies his request.
The marshal orders the door forced down.
The press is hauled outside and broken;
the type piled in the street.
Mr. Higbee and his cohorts curse
the marshal and all who watch.
They threaten the Prophet's life,
yell he is endangered by this deed.
Libelous papers, pamphlets of lies
become flames curling smoke
toward heaven
where true mercy is meted out.

With ashes still glowing,
we march to the Mansion House
to give the Prophet our report.

The author of this poem is **Alexander Neibaur** *who is also the author of the hymn "Come Thou Glorious Day of Promise." see L.D.S. Hymn Books, current. The strong Hebraic character of the above poem will appear to the reader.*

Lamentation

Of a Jew Among the Afflicted and Mourning Sons and Daughters of Zion, at the Assassination of the Two Chieftains in Israel, Joseph and Hyrum Smith.

Blessed the people knowing the shout of Jehovah,
In the light of his countenance they will walk.
How can we, a people in sackcloth,
Open our lips before thee?
They have rejected and slain our leaders,
Thine anointed ones.
Our eyes are dim, our hearts heavy;
No place of refuge being left,
Redeem the people that in thee only trusts;
There is none to stand between and inquire;
Thou art our helper,
The refuge of Israel in time of trouble.
O look in righteousness upon thy faithful servants,
Who have laid bare their lives unto death,
Not withholding their bodies;
Being betrayed by false brethren, and
    their lives cut off,
Forbidding their will before thine;
Having sanctified thy great name,
Never polluting it;
Ready for a sacrifice;—standing in the breach,
Tried, proved and found perfect,
To save the blood of the fathers;
Their children, brothers, and sisters;
Adding theirs unto those who are gone before them;
Sanctifying thy holy and great name upon the earth;
Cover and conceal not their blood.
Give ear unto their cries until thou lookest

And shewest down from heaven—taking vengeance
And avenging their blood—avenging thy people and
    thy law,
According to thy promises made
Unto our forefathers, Abraham, Isaac and Jacob.
Hasten the acceptable and redeeming year;
Shadday; remember unto us thy covenants;
All this heaviness has reached us;
Can anyone be formed to declare
What has befallen us?
All this we bear, and the name of our God
We will not forget, nor deny,
The "Hebrews' God" he is called,
Thou are clothed with righteousness,
But we are vile.
Come not in judgment with us.
Before thee nothing living is justified by
    their works.
But be with us as thou wast with our fathers.
Help us, O Father; unto thee
We will lift our souls,
Our hearts in our hands;
We look to heaven,
Lifting our eyes unto the mountains,
From whence cometh our help.
Turn away thine anger,
That we be not spoiled.
O return and leave a blessing behind thee.

Times and Seasons, vol. v. p. 591.
History of the Church, Vol. VII, p. 191

Battle of Nauvoo

Sept 11 1844 Mob moved North towards Wm Laws field firing 35 canon balls myself being placed in a corn field opposite Hyrams farm to spring a mine 2 forts erected in the Night Sept 12 Mob makes a Attak to get into Nauvoo Br Wm Anderson & Br Morris belonging to the 5 quorum of 70 being shot Br Whithead & 2 others woundet the Mob being Repellet with a Number of Woundet

Ellen quiets her children huddled around her skirts.
Outside she sees soldiers showing no regard
for their garden greens. Yesterday they broke down
the fence, trampled beans and cabbages.
Today their horses munch carrot tops and corn stalks.

Their leader rides his horse up to the door,
dismounts, drawn sword in hand.
Alexander stretches his thin frame,
filling the doorway, facing the soldier who asks,
"Were you in the fight yesterday?"

"I was." Ellen hears the strength in his reply.

"Have you a gun?" the soldier asks.

"I have." Ellen watches; her husband doesn't budge.
She remembers vividly the wails
of sisters whose husbands were shot.

"Bring it to me!" the soldier demands.

Ellen feels 10-year-old Joseph William squirm,
wanting to move forward to get a better view.
She places her hand firmly on his arm.
They hear, *"The general wants every gun
that was in that fight."*

Ellen gulps in air but will not let her children
see her fright. She sees Alexander stand
as firm as beech trees yesterday while cannons
belched fumes, woke babies, made women cringe.

"If you want my gun, you find it," her husband says.
She notes how his voice fills with disdain.
She can scarcely breathe.

Alexander waits to see how the soldier reacts,
then quickly adds, *"Take me to your general."*
His voice is firm, his words like cannon reports.
"I am quite willing to see him."
Only then does Ellen see him move.

Alexander steps two paces forward,
flashes the soldier a Masonic sign.
The soldier acknowledges, turns,
drops his sword inside its sheath,
mounts his horse, speaks quietly to his men,
leads them from the family's garden spot.

Laying the Nauvoo Temple Capstone

May 24, 1845 top stone of the Temple laid

My family joins many saints assembled to witness
the laying of the Temple capstone.
In cool of early morning, the brass band blasts
music of the "Nightingale" into the air.
At 6:08 Brother William Player spreads the mortar.

Silence prevails; even our children sense the magnificence
of this moment as the stone is lifted to its place.
Brother Brigham steps on the stone, fits it precisely
to its position with the large beetle.
At twenty-two minutes past six, he calls,
"The capstone is set!"
The band plays the "Capstone March"
composed for the occasion by Brother William Pitt.

"The last stone is now laid upon the Temple,"
Brother Brigham states, *"and I pray the Almighty
in the name of Jesus to defend us in this place
and sustain us until the Temple is finished
and we have all got our endowments."*

*"Hosanna, Hosanna, to God
and the Lamb, Amen, Amen, and Amen."*
We repeat the chant three times, a roar of joy
from our hearts spills into our voices.

"So let it be, O Lord Almighty,"
Brother Brigham prays,
*"This is the seventh day of the week
or the Jewish Sabbath. It is the day
on which the Almighty finished his work
and rested from his labors.
We have finished the walls of the Temple
and we may rest today from our labors."*

Down by the River's Verdant Side

Somberly ♩=54
Alex Neibaur

1. Down by the river's verdant side, Low by the solitary tide, There, while the peaceful waters slept, We pensively sat down and wept, And on the bending willows hung Our silent harps through grief unstrung.
2. For they who wasted Zion's bowers And laid in dust her ruined towers In scorn their weary slaves desire To strike the chords of Israel's lyre, And in their impious ears to sing The sacred songs to Zion's King.
3. How shall we tune those lofty strains On Babylon's polluted plains, When low in ruin on the earth Remains the place that gave us birth, And stern destruction's iron hand Still sways our desolated land.
4. O never shall our harps awake, Laid in the dust for Zion's sake. Forever on the willows hung, Their music hushed; their chords unstrung; Lost Zion! city of our God, While groaning 'neath the tyrant's rod.

5 Still mould'ring lie thy leveled walls
And ruin stalks along thy halls.
And brooding o'er thy ruined towers
Such desolation sternly lowers,
That when we muse upon thy woe,
The gushing tears of sorrow flow!

6 And while we toil through wretched life
And drink the bitter cup of strife,
Until we yield our weary breath,
And sleep released from woe in death,
Will Zion in our memory stand—
Our lost, our ruined native land.

Come, Thou Glorious Day of Promise
(Choir)

Alex Neibaur
A. C. Smyth

With breadth ♩=63

1. Come, thou glo-rious day of prom-ise; Come and spread thy cheer-ful ray When the scat-tered sheep of Is-rael Shall no long-er go a-stray; When ho-san-nas, When ho-san-nas With u-nit-ed voice they'll cry.

2. Lord, how long wilt thou be an-gry? Shall thy wrath for-ev-er burn? Rise, re-deem thine an-cient peo-ple; Their trans-gres-sions from them turn; King of Is-rael, King of Is-rael, Come and set thy peo-ple free.

3. Oh, that soon thou wouldst to Ja-cob Thy en-live-ning Spir-it send! Of their un-be-lief and mis-er-y Make, O Lord, a speed-y end. Lord, Mes-si-ah! Lord, Mes-si-ah! Prince of Peace o'er Is-rael reign.

On To Zion

went to Missoury to get a fit out [outfit] for the Mountains...

Alexander Neibaur

Dentistry in Farmington, Iowa

(1846)

The men wear guns upon their hips;
their clothes are soiled, their bodies smell,
and both men reek from alcohol.
*"I hear you are a dentist here.
My teeth are causing me great pain."*
The dentist says, *"Put down your gun.
I'll look to see what's troubling you.
I'm glad to help you if I can."*

"You've got two yawning cavities,"
the dentist tells the man. *"I'll fill
the two worst ones for you; there's more
that can be done another day."*
The hand drill makes the patient wince
as cavity edges are smoothed.
He swears out loud, his vulgar words
continue, while the dentist mix-

es silver nitrate for the fill.
"Where are you from?" the patient asks.
"I'm from Nauvoo," the dentist says.
"Are you a Joe Smith follower?"
The patient's face burns burly red,
then he begins a long tirade
of calling names. *"Gold-digger Smith
got his reward–we killed that guy!"*

Like water from a turned-on pump,
blasphemous words pour from his lips.
"Stop that right now!" the doctor says.
*"I will not hear you talk that way!
The Prophet was a man of God
who did no wrong, but still was killed."*
The patient stands and grabs his gun,
pulls back the hammer, aims and shoots.

Six times he pulls the trigger in;
six times it merely clicks and moves.
The patient swears,"*Sonuvabitch!*"
then throws his gun down to the floor.
His brother steps into the room.
"*What is the trouble here?*" he asks.
"*Why, that damn gun just wouldn't work!*"
The brother picks it from the floor.

He pulls the trigger. Loud reports
sends six straight bullets out the door.
"*I cannot see a problem here.*
I wonder just what ailed your hand."
He shrugs and then hands back the gun.
The patient hears the Doctor say,
"*My guardian angel stood by me*
to keep my blood from being spilled."

Delivery at Winter Quarters

Dec 12 1847 my Wife confined child dead
the Power of God & the Priesthood made bare in a Wonderfull manner
praised be the Lord God of Israel for his Mercys towards me & mine I want
my children to Remember this day

Ellen agonizes through labor pains,
each one as severe as a turning sword.
Her memory brings back pain endured
in seven earlier births, recalls instead the joy
those new babies brought. Between the pains, she sees
icicles hanging from the eaves,
snow falling, hears the howling winds.

The task demands her thoughts. She concentrates
on breathing, on bearing down, exerting that thrust
delivery requires. The midwife tells her
the baby's nearly here. She grips bed posts, groans,
bears down until the head is through.
Another push brings shoulders,
arms, torso, legs. *"It's a girl."*

Ellen closes her eyes to rest, relieved,
senses hearing only the spatting of hand
on flesh, the hurried movements
in the room, no cries. She musters energy,
raises her head, *"Is she all right?"*

In the dimness of coal oil lamp glow,
she cannot see clearly what the midwife does.
No answer comes, only the shuffling of feet.
Ellen hears whining of bitter wind inside her head,
demands, *"Is she all right?"* This time the midwife speaks,
"I can't get her to breathe."

The agony within those words
becomes a dagger of ice freezing Ellen's heart.

A False Start

May 18, 1848 went to Fort Kearny Returnt Ap 30 Preparet for the journey to the Great Salt Lake got 2 waggens one yoke of Oxen from Widow Knight one yoke of Oxen of Br Joseph Young Started from Winter Quarters May 20 went about 2 miles going up a Hill the falls tounge [false tongue] split the Waggon run bak upset broke one hind weel [wheel] forcet to Return to Winterquarter

With two wagons, one borrowed from Widow Knight,
and a yoke of oxen, my family starts from Winter Quarters.
Joseph William, now 13, handles the oxen team.
Isaac, at 9 years, helps feed and harness,
hook up, tie down.
The morning air is brisk, excitement
hovers near, but we push it aside.
We've heard the trek is long.
My wife helps whenever she can,
but our three little ones require constant care.

The oxen keep a steady pace.
Barely two miles from our starting place,
the oxen strain on the uphill pull.
The false tongue of the wagon splits.
The oxen bolt ahead, dragging the loose tongue.
Double-trees, still attached, jingle freely
near their hooves. Joseph sets the wagon brake,
jumps off, stays with the team, calls ahead to me.

I hurry back in time to see the wagon
rolling downhill in spite of brakes.
The uneven road topples the wagon
on its side. My family scramble free,
run to my protecting arms.
Other drivers come to help.
They right the wagon, but it stands askew.
The hind wheel took more weight
than it could bear.

Lure of Gooseberry Pie

June 1 1847 ...Sister Susan Miller & Rilens going a gooseberrying Strayed and lost their way being out all Night Some men going in Search meeting with them 3 miles from camp...

Green gooseberries tantalize
two ladies' lips. They can taste
the tartness of the berries sweetened into pie.
With buckets on their arms,
they follow wild gooseberry paths,
plunking green globes repeatedly
into tin pails. They pick one bush,
move on, thoughts full of gooseberry pies
they will share when they return.

Each bush leads to another farther on.
The women keep the next berry bush,
not camp, in sight, do not realize
how far they've gone. Soon each rolling hill
looks like the one before.
They cannot remember over which one
they came, nor how to retrace their way.
Dusk diminishes to dark.
They huddle together,
full pails of berries beneath a bush.

They kneel in prayer and wait,
talking quietly as hours pass.
They shout an answer when they hear
their men's loud calls, see lanterns waving.
Forgetting gooseberries in pails beneath the bush,
they run to waiting arms.

Prairie Music

Oxen hooves plod
on hardened sod,
a strained melody
across prairie.
Harnesses tweak
a rasping sque-eak;
soft ting-a-ling,
double-trees sing.
Oi-r-nk, axles grunt.
Wooden wheels stunt
sagebrush and pass
onto crushed grass.
The canvas chants
when wagon slants
through gullies and
pockets of sand,
miniature bowls
of prairie dog holes.
Rocks and piled mud
make contents thud;
huge skillets bang
walls where they hang.
Campfires crack,
travelers snack,
lulled off to sleep
while hoot owls keep
vigil; the wings
of cricket sings
a drummed lullaby;
pioneers sigh.

Buffalo On The Prairie

Aug 4 1848 ...Br Gates having killt a Buffalo gone out to fetch in...6 ...Br Gates having sent word that there was part of a Buffalo for our Company...7 fine breezy morn camp at Mineral Springs my watch out of order at a loss for the time of day shot a Buffalo

We see the teeming herds on the plateau,
a cloud of dust of such immensity.
I want to say *I killt a buffalo.*

They seem to move in measured steps, quite slow,
and yet, I've heard of their ferocity.
We see the teeming herds on the plateau

but can't get near; they seem to know
and are imbued with great agility.
I want to say *I killt a buffalo.*

We went out hunting and I shot a doe,
but do not think I make apology.
We see the teeming herds on the plateau;

my hunting group follows their steady flow
along the plains, brown dust quite billowy.
I want to say *I killt a buffalo.*

We sight a bull alone; it's touch and go.
I raise my gun, a little fidgety.
We left the teeming herds on the plateau.
Rejoice! Today I killt a buffalo.

In The Great Salt Lake Valley

Sept. 24, 1848 fine cool morn reacht the Valy in the Afternoon a fine Looking country...

Alexander Neibaur

Winter 1848

Dec 4 1848 cold day [5-6-7 cold days [8 moderate 9 cold 10-11 Snow 12 & 13 very Stormy & cold 14 heavy wind tent blown down 15 very cold & Snow 16 windy tent down again [17 heavy Snow at night

Winds howl like hungry wolves around canvas walls.
The family of nine huddles in their tent,
cannot see snow twisting, white on white.
Thin canvas deflects the wind,
does not deter its relentless four-day chill.

The family pushes weighted snow from their sagging shield.
Mother warms tiny fingers inside her palms,
kisses children's cheeks,
rewraps the baby who kicks free from her quilt.
One globed lantern sheds thin light within.
A gusting wind flails the canvas walls,
uproots pegs from frozen ground, flattens the heavy tarp.

In unison all arms lift, upholding the tent.
"Come quickly!" Father calls.
Young sons, 13 and 9, follow into the biting wind.
Mother leaves her 11-year-old to comfort
the huddled crying young.
Stretching one rope at a time,
men and Mother combat the winds,
turn faces from pelting ice.
Father pounds new stakes into frozen earth.
The canvas pulls taut.

Inside, he hugs his sons, gathers,
comforts his little ones.
Candles offer meager heat and light
while blizzards whirl outside.

The young need more warmth than candle glow,
their bodies hunger for more than bread and milk.
They whimper into mournful winds.
Pegs uproot once more, flatten the tent.
Candles are quickly doffed
to quell their flames in straw.
"Stay inside."
Parents slip into the bitter wind.

> One hundred and fifty years later,
> in my heat-regulated room,
> I watch whirling snows, see tree branches
> bend in whistling winds,
> recall winter 1848, shiver for them.

And God Set Rainbows In The Heavens

May 20, 1849 Rainy day May 21 Wife confinet of a little Girl

I wipe my forearm across my brow.
Rain rivers down adobes below unglazed windows.
A variety of spots drip constantly from the roof.
Alexander and Joseph spent all winter making bricks
to create this haven from storms.
Between labor pains I think on the joy
of putting that tent away, though it sheltered nine of us
here in the Valley and traveling from Nauvoo.

Newborn Leah was nineteen days old
when we were forced to leave. It rained then, too.
How difficult to nurse or change a baby
with rain pouring down,
our only shelter the wagon bed.
Today's adobes ward off most of the rain
unless it persists in wearing them away.

Ooh, that pain's sharp! I let thoughts of rain run off,
grab pillars of the new bed Alexander made
of logs strung firm with ropes. A feather bed adds a luxury
so different from hard ground on the trek west.
These labor pains cannot be harder to endure
than that long walk, encouraging our tiny ones along.

I close my eyes to rest, hear the persisting rain.
My midwife side-steps rivulets running beneath my bed.
My childbirth two years ago was also on a stormy day.
Those December pains were as severe as these,
yet rewards of birthing were removed.
We shared the Bullock family's Winter Quarters home.
All offered empathy when stillborn Rachel
joined her brother Isaac who's been nine years with God.

Today I push a new child forth,
praying God will let this one live,
that it will be strong enough for Zion.
Provisions for this large family have been sparse
these eight months here.
Love abounds, strengthens me.
Each pain increases its power. Ah, it subsides.

I almost hate to close my eyes.
Thoughts whirl like the wind pushing this rain.
I hear its pattering, the constant streams
running inside and out. I look toward the gray.
God promised no more Noah storms,
set rainbows in the sky to comfort us.

Renewed, I endure breathtaking bearing-down pains,
hear the longed-for cry of life,
see my daughter raised up, red.
They bring Sarah Ellen to cuddle in my arms,
rewards of birth prismatic,
joyful as rainbows.

Letters From Silicia

Sep 28 1852 Received a letter from my Father & my Widowed Sister Bertha Informing me that they wish to come to America, but not having the Means to come I went to see Governor Brigham Young about their coming by England with the Perpetual Emigration Company, had their names put down, send a letter by the way of Liverpool to Germany also one to Manchester to my Brother David & one to New York to my Brother Adolf:

I remember how I reread my father's words.
He and my sister want to come
to America, but have no funds.
I went to Brother Brigham immediately
to put their names on the list for help
from the Perpetual Emigration Fund.

That was two years ago. Each letter
makes me rejoice they still want to come.
My heart breaks anew as letters only arrive.
Time presses. I still am unable to help.
Letters renew our hopes of an embrace.
They're a bridge to span the gap of loneliness.

Mr. Julius Brooks informed me he had seen my father
doing well in Silicia before Brooks came here.
I want Father here, not just reports of him.
Although I exchange letters with my brother Adolf
in New York, he writes he cannot help.

> Father's letter from Warmbrun, Silicia today
> fills me with sorrow to read of Adolf's death.
> I cannot bear to think the next letter from my kin
> might contain similar news about Father or other family.

Oh, Lord God of Israel,
you answer so many prayers for me,
why can your ears not hear this fervent plea?

Sharing with Strangers

Oct 5 1856 Sunday Meeting President Young called for 60 mule & horse teams - 40 young men to go out with 12 tons of flour to bring in the Saints: also for Donations in Shoes Clothing & Blankets for the Saints, the Br & Sisters came forward liberally

Ellen holds her newly knitted stockings,
pleased with their perfect blue and white stripes.
"These will go well with my new shoes."
They are hard items to come by of late.

A knock on the door sends curious children to see who calls.
President Brigham Young's messenger requests,
"*shoes, socks, clothing of any kind,
any items that can be spared for the incoming Saints.*"

Alexander despairs, "*We have nothing to give.*"
Ellen recalls how rocks pierced her worn shoes on her trek west.
She shivers as if a cool canyon breeze blew past
like those felt crossing the Divide or the Wasatch range.

She says, "*We must give something.*" She sits,
removes new shoes, pulls off long blue
and white stockings, holds them all
for a minute to her breast, hands them to the messenger.

"*It's the least I can do,*" she tells her children.
She finds rags, wraps her feet against October's cold ground,
draws her children close to express her love,
reminds them she is blessed.

Word spreads, "*The Saints are coming in.
All must turn out.*" Ellen re-wraps her feet,
joins the welcomers. She spies a woman
wearing blue and white, sees her shiny shoes.

The woman walks nearby, calls Ellen by name.
She is a friend from Preston years before.

Shabbot Text

Dec 1, 1854 taken sick 2-3 continued sick Brigham Young preacht concerning the Jews–no Jew coming in the Church would Remain faithfull Brother Neibaur as a jew has changed his jewish Blood. there is not a smallest particle of the Blood of a jew in him...

Alexander has been six years in the Valley when he takes sick,
has to miss the Sunday services. Word comes quickly
of Brother Brigham's text. *"No Jew coming in the church,"*
the Governor states, *"would remain true. Brother Neibaur
has not the smallest particle of Jewish blood in him."*

Alexander rants about Brigham's words, feels the wrath
his father felt when told his son converted
from Jewish faith. Alexander tried to help his father
understand, could not. Now Brother Brigham states
this Jewish blood, which endured the walk across the plains,
has not the stamina to maintain his faith.

Alexander recalls that as a student in dentistry, he studied hard.
His Bar Mitzvah happiness filled the gaps
of loneliness he felt so far from home,
from those he loved. He consoled himself
his family would welcome him after graduation day.
Father accepted his choice of dentistry
rather than rabbinical school.

England offered more than Prussia
in dental trade. Still home tugged at his heart–
Mother, Father, Shabbot at sundown,
candles being lit, Father's tenor chant.
Memories sustain him through school.

He fell in love with an "estimable" English maid
who staunchly embraced Christian ways.
He loved her, wanted to marry her,
knew his mother's heart would break if he married
out of Jewish faith. His father would not accept
such news with grace. He tried to think of ways
to lessen their ache, found none. He married,
but not beneath a canopy.

He joined the Mormons, sailed to America,
found the prophet, land of his own, the fellowship
of kindred souls. Still, he recalls Passovers, Hanukkahs,
traditional Jewish rites, but his kin are far
away. What few letters he receives are strained;
the news, and love, too sparse.

Mobs killed the prophet, burned Nauvoo homes.
Forced to leave, go west, as the prophet foretold
they would before his death, Alexander followed Brigham
here, only to be accused of shallow faith.
Yes, he cannot wait to talk with Brigham Young.

"*Truth is,*" said Brother Brigham, "*as a convert,
you adopted Ephraim's line.*" Alexander fails to see his point.
"*As one of us, on Ephraim's line, you are no longer Jew,
but there are few Saints who have more faith than you.*"
Alexander mumbles, pleased by the compliment,
but still does not agree he's changed his Jewish blood.

Like the Seagulls

March 8 1856 plant winsor beans onion beets 21 drilled wheat on City lot Sowet Tomato 27 Musk & Water Melon Beats...Apr16 plant Corn & Squash & Cucumbers on city lot 19 began to plant potatoes corn & Squash at 5 acre lot
May 3 1856 Hard times for something to eat

Last year the grasshoppers swarmed,
a black cloud of doom,
attacking every green leaf
with voracious appetites.
They were underfoot, in our faces, our hair,
drowning in our water pails, leaping
into our beds. Even after the seagulls
devoured millions of them in the fields,
we found them everywhere, swept them,
crunching beneath our feet.

We planted again, but harvests were small.
My children don't complain about repeated
breakfasts of bran mush, occasional suppers
of sego root soup, but mostly pigweed greens.
Little Sarah's six-year-old lips curl in disgust,
but she butters the bitter greens, forces them
through her lips, only to excuse herself.
She runs behind the house, heaves
them back to the soil–where they belong.

I hear her siblings taunt her, saying
she's like the seagulls, regurgitating greens.
I chastise them, knowing she often faints
from lack of food. She quietly asks,
"Mama, must I eat these again?"

I promise her early peas, new potatoes,
corn, squash, muskmelons and buttered beets
her father's planted
if she can endure till harvest time.

Brighton Camp, Cottonwood Canyon, July 24, 1857

July 22 going in Cotton wood Kaniyon to celebrate the entrance of the Pioneers in the Valey = my wheat [23 Br Judson Stoddart who ought to have brought the Eastern Mail returnt without a Mail the General Government refusing to send the Mail

Our ten-year celebration starts tonight.
Many Saints have journeyed far to celebrate
in homes sheltered by this Wasatch Mountain range.
Before our family left Salt Lake for the canyon, news came
the government refuses to send out our Territory mail.
That news chills me just as cool air shivers my skin.

In these ten years, we've sought peace, a place to worship,
wanting those same rights other citizens enjoy.
Brother Brigham says those who send untruths
back to the States are *"infernal scoundrels."*
He denies their rumors that only Mormons are welcome here.

We gather round the campfire as night draws down.
We hear approaching horses' hooves, a gun's report.
Brother Parley Pratt rides in, fires his gun toward the stars.
He tells Brother Brigham, loud enough for all to hear,
*"Johnston's Army's on its way! They intend to strip away
our rights—remove Brother Brigham as Governor."*

Murmurs reach a deafening level as we recall
the mobs, the guns, the cannons, the martyrdom
of the Prophet Joseph and Hyrum Smith, killings
at Haun's Mill, the burnings in Nauvoo,
arrests of our good men. Brother Brigham says,

*"We'll burn our homes, our barns. Let nothing stand
for them to conquer, to use, or to enjoy."*
All shout acclaim. Memories are still fresh
of being driven out before, of sufferings, starvation
on the trails. All agree, if we must lose
our homes again, we will leave nothing here!
Let Johnston's Army come. We are prepared to fight.

Torches for the City

Oct 7 1857 conf dismis by Pr: B. Young Forth Bridger & Supply burnt by the Brethren heavy Rain at night Oct 8 an Express brought word that Br Lot Smith hath burned 51 waggons & their loading belonging to the U.S.

In Salt Lake Valley we pack our things, round up our livestock,
leave for Provo, but this time, we place sawdust and straw
about, ready to be torched by guards who stay behind.
Our homes will not be ready occupancy
for mobbers driving us away.

>President Young dismissed Conference,
>admonished us to live exemplary lives.
>He announced both Forts Bridger and Supply
>had been burned by our troops.

My son Isaac has been at outposts for a month.
An Express brought word Brother Lot Smith burned 51 wagons
which were bringing in much-needed supplies for Johnston's
army pressing to our valley.
Another rider reports more wagons torched,
prairie fires deliberately set, destroying grasses
needed for feed for Army stock.

In Provo, we cheer to learn the Army's request for replacements
was denied, that Congressmen think the Utah War
a gross mismanagement of funds and men.
President Buchanan offers peace, amnesty to those
involved in "insurrection" here. He strips
President Young of his political seat, bestows it
on Alfred Cummings, a man opposed to us.

President Young agrees Johnston's army of hungry men
can come to the valley, providing
they remain twenty miles from settlements.

We see their encampments to the west as we go home.

Contemplations

Br Neibaur stands fairer than ever, and I wish I could say as much of every one in my ward as I can say of Br Neibaur and his family.

Bishop Wooley, 13th Ward January 1862

I do not pen these lines but for the Gratification of my Posterity Bearing to them and unto all who may Read these few lines my Testimony that Joseph Smith was a Prophet of the Lord, the things spoken of in the Bible, Book of Mormon, & Sealt with the Blood of the Martyrs at Carthage Jail, Ill etc are true...
    Alexander Neibaur's Personal Testimony Given in 1869

Father, Was It Worth It All?*

Yes, my son, and more,
for I have seen my Savior.
I have seen the prints in His hands.
I know Jesus is the Son of God.
I know his work is true,
and Joseph Smith was a Prophet of God.

I would suffer it all
and more, far more
than I have suffered
for that knowledge,
even to the laying down
of my body on the plains
for the wolves to devour.

My prayer is that my posterity
might walk in the way of righteousness.
               Amen.

Alexander's response to his son prior to his death in December 1883

Ethereal Pressure

Whether in groups
or in solitaire, your name emerges.
I feel your wishes pressing thoughts
into my awareness as firmly as your hat
with its peculiar hole found its place
on your head when you went out.
Your whiskered face focuses
into my ongoing life
still intermixing with memories of you.

The only release valve
is my pen to the page,
pushing pent-up phrases
beyond the confines of storage,
unearthing tales told
but ghosted through living.
This inner dream can be quieted
only by inking words,
etching them as if in stone.

Your stilled voice breaks
through ethereal space,
whispers,
sends me on urgent tangents
to do your bidding,
to do for you after death
things I could not do for you in life.

Next Year in Jerusalem

Generations bring changes
and forgettings. New beliefs
obliterate Passover ceremonies
except for the final chanted phrase,
lingering generations deep,
"Next year in Jerusalem!"

My grandmother never ate a Passover meal
nor celebrated Hanukkah with her kin.
*"Oh, if I could go one day
to Jerusalem,"* Great-Grandma said,
*"but these weary legs won't take me.
This worn body cannot cross the miles
to take me* Home *to Israel."*

Home to Israel was her desire,
not where she was born.
Her father and grandfather
were Prussian Jews, German, French.
Their chanted dream seemed transmitted
through their genes,
deeply impacted,
"Next year in Jerusalem!"

Dedication:
Orson Hyde Park, Jerusalem, Israel

(October 24, 1979)

The Moslem call to prayer was my alarm;
my eyes would not return to sleep.

Spectators, like myself at the meditation park,
line the path.   My grandkids sit two rows away,
my daughter by my side. My grandma,
who dreamed of Israel, is here in memory.

The park is damp from evening rain;
slick, red clay adheres to everything.
Flags of Israel and USA flutter
in Kidron Valley breeze.
Jerusalem reflects the morning sun.

I start to speak; my throat constricts.
My eyes streak makeup on my aging cheeks.
I look away to flying flags, take deep breaths.
My daughter holds my hand.

The waiting congregation sings a hymn.
The hillside reverberates the melody.
"Israel, Israel, God is calling..."
Grandma, I sing in your behalf.
Please sing along with me.
"We thank Thee, oh God, for a prophet..."

He and his procession pass,
he shakes my grandson's hand.
"You help build our Jerusalem;"
Mayor Kollek says, *"we'll help
build yours."* The aging prophet prays;
his former weakened voice
resonant, clear.

Walk in the Women's Center Garden, Nauvoo

Spirits of mothers,
my extended mothers,
touch my shoulders,
encircle me
as I cross red bricks leading to statues
of women in loving poses,
showing varied ways mothers give love.

Bird trills echo in tree tops.
Reverence hovers here.
Love distills
from beloved mothers
whose memories I revere,
who once kept vigil here.
Similar birds sang when you lived in Nauvoo,
gave birth, showed your children love.

Before being driven west, you planted seeds,
harvested crops, preserved fruits,
walked these streets drenched in sunshine like today.

Your names are preserved inside
the building's cornerstone, a tribute
to your convictions, strength, and stamina.

Like the birds, I trill
the memories of you.

Continuum of Green

(Observation in 1997)

I sit in shelter of umber rocks
on a sweltering spring day.
From atop Mount Olympus I see
the valley from the eagle's view.
I piece together its composite parts starting
where Brigham said, "This is the Place,"
to Ensign Peak, to snow-capped Oquirrhs on the west,
to the Big and Little Cottonwoods,
wooded canyons on the east.

I rejoice that pioneer men stayed, planted
and plowed, built adobes, in spite of weary wives
who volunteered to walk another thousand
miles rather than stay in a valley with no trees,
no shelter from constant August heat,
no break against winter's insistent winds.

Saplings, planted after peas and corn were
flourishing, have stood through heat and cold
of the desert's seasonal blossoming,
as did those hardy pioneers who created
this greenery spreading miles wide.

Communities nest between highway arteries.
Neighborhood trees form a continuum
of green humping tall enough
to obscure mansions sheltered beneath them.
Temple spires built by pioneers
and tall buildings of modern design
surround the Capitol. As far as an eagle's eye sees,
where once wheat, barley and potatoes grew,
fields of houses spread in all directions
shaded by all varieties of trees.

In Their Shadow

Wagons roll West from Nauvoo
one hundred fifty years following the first forced trek.
These modern men, women and children, dress
in period clothes, some have period wagons,
traverse trails and byways blazed decades before.
As in those days, horses and mules pull their rigs.
Modern trekkers eat dust, wade in mud,
ford swift streams, swat mosquitos and flies,
burn from the sun, shiver in the cold.

In hamlets of fifty people or cities with thousands,
modern trekkers are greeted with welcoming waves,
honking horns, treated to community barbecues.
Fast food suppliers, Coca-Cola trucks and Porta-Potties
fill their immediate needs. Their predecessors
were greeted by Indian raiding parties, rattlesnakes,
hoot owls, coyotes. They cooked their meals
on dry buffalo chips, when they were found.

Today's highways fill with 18-wheelers zooming past,
spooking wagon train horses, but wagonmasters
keep control, know the hay wagon pulls into camp
at night laden with alfalfa. These trekkers
don't have grass burned ahead of them by Indians
who fear the wagons will chase off their buffalo.

Souls of pioneer trekkers seemed strengthened
when the soles of their only shoes wore through.
Up Rocky Ridge, they would have loved a pair
of modern walking shoes.

Early Saints were driven from their homes
by mandates from counties and governors.
Today's Saints are welcomed by governors
of each state they cross. They recognize
these Saints are driven by a desire to relive
an ancestor's dream, to prove their own mettle
in this modern world, that in making the trek,
they rededicate themselves to Zion.

FAMILY GROUP RECORD

HUSBAND Alexander NEIBAUR (Dentist)

Born	8 Jan 1828	Place: Ehrenbreitstein, Rheinland, Prussia
Chr.	16 Sept 1834	Place: Chorley, Lancashire, England
Mar.		Place: Salt Lake City, Salt Lake, Utah
Died	15 Dec 1883	Place: Salt Lake City, Salt Lake, Utah
Bur.		Place: Salt Lake City Cem., Salt Lake City, Utah

HUSBAND'S FATHER: Joseph Nathan NEIBAUR MOTHER: Rebecca Peretz SAMUEL
HUSBAND'S OTHER WIVES: md (2) 8 Nov 1852 Ann (WALTON) CLEMENTS (3) 1 Sep 1871 Elizabeth LILLEY

WIFE Ellen Bannister BREAKELL

Born	28 Feb 1811	Place: Longton, Lancashire, England
Chr.	31 Mar 1811	Place:
Died	14 Dec 1870	Place: Salt Lake City, Salt Lake, Utah
Bur.		Place: Salt Lake City Cem., Salt Lake City, Utah

WIFE'S FATHER: Richard BREAKELL MOTHER: Alice BANNISTER

CHILDREN

Sex	Children (in order of birth)	When Born (Day Month Year)	Where Born (Town)	(County)	(State or Country)	Date of First Marriage — To Whom	Day Month Year When Died	Baptized	Endowed	Sealed to Parents
M	1. Joseph William NEIBAUR	6 Jan 1835 chr. Feb 1835	Preston	Lancs	Eng.	13 Jan 1857 Elizabeth CRANSHAW	2 May 1927	31 Oct 1852	1 Nov 1848	2 Nov 1852 NV EH
F	2. Margaret B.	20 Feb 1836 chr 29 Apr 1836	"	"	"		29 Jan 1928	"	1 Nov 1848	2 Nov 1852 EH
M	3. Isaac (alias Peretz Samuel)	7 Jan 1838 chr 15 Jan 1838	"	"	"	3/5 Shype 1856 William MILLER	2 Jan 1839	child		20 Aug 1954 EH
M	4. Isaac	30 Mar 1839	"	"	"	22 Jan 1863 Emily HOLLAND	abt 1899	15 Mar 1965	21 Aug 1857	20 Aug 1954 EH
F	5. Alice Breakell	22 May 1841	Nauvoo	Hancock	Ill.	2 Apr 1859 Morris Dayid ROSENBAUM	13 Mar 1914	31 Oct 1852	21 Aug 1857	20 Aug 1954 EH
F	6. Bertha Breakell	14 Dec 1842	"	"	"	9 Nov 1862 Levy FANSBURN		31 Oct 1852	19 Oct 1867	20 Aug 1954 EH
M	7. Hyrum Smith	30 Nov 1844	"	"	"	14 Jan 1866 Jane Harriett SPRIGGS	6 Oct 1934	29 Oct 1854	19 Jan 1867	20 Aug 1954 EH
F	8. Leah Breakell	29 Aug 1846	"	"	"	23 May 1866 Adam Wilroy PAUL		29 Oct 1854	1 Dec 1866	BIC EH
F	9. Rachel	12 Dec 1847	Winter Quarters (now Omaha)	Douglas	Neb.	---	Stillborn	child	child	BIC
F	10. Sarah Ellen Breakell	21 May 1849	Salt Lake City	Salt Lake	Utah	16 Nov 1867 John S. SMITH (alias O'BRIEN)	1928	19 Mar 1857	16 Nov 1867	BIC EH
F	11. Rebecca Ann Breakell	30 Mar 1851	"	"	"	3 Mar 1869 Charles Wilson NIBLEY		30 Mar 1859	30 Mar 1869	BIC

OTHER MARRIAGES: child #1 md (2) child #6 md (2)

NECESSARY EXPLANATIONS
marr. date of child #2 from Patron Sheets of LDS Archives (Junkerfield)

1873 Charles Patman Cunningham FILLMORE

SOURCES OF INFORMATION
1. Family Bible of Alexander Neibaur 2. Chorley PR 3. Longton PR
4. Death Certificates (Ellen, wife, children 2, 5, 7, 10, 11, 13, 14)
5. Preston PR 6. Annual report Paris, 1st wound death of child #1
7. Nauvoo Temple (Priesthood Seventies Record from Early Church Info. File (bpt. of Alex) 9. Early Church Info. File for bpt. of wife
G'd children # 1, 2, 5, 6, 10. SLC 13th wd Rec. bpt. of 7, 8, 13.

Family Group Record

HUSBAND Alexander NEIBAUR (Sheet #2)

CHILDREN Sex / List each child in order of birth / Given Names	SURNAME	WHEN BORN DAY MONTH YEAR	WHERE BORN TOWN	COUNTY	STATE OR COUNTRY	DATE OF FIRST MARRIAGE / TO WHOM	WHEN DIED MONTH DAY YEAR	BAPTIZED (date)	ENDOWED (date)	SEALED (date and place) CHILDREN TO PARENTS
12 F	Mary Esther NEIBAUR	4 Dec 1852	Salt Lake City	Salt Lake	Ut.		30 Dec 1852	child	child	B/C
13 F	Matilda Isabella "	30 Jan 1854	"	"	"	20 Dec 1872 / to William WORDEN	7 Dec 1921	4 Sep 1861	30 May 1894 St.	B/C
14 M	Nathan Alexander "	14 Sep 1855	"	"	"	Georgiana CLYDE	15 July 1942	2 June 1864	10 June 1923 AZ	B/C

OTHER MARRIAGES
Child #13 md(2) 17 Feb 1894 John Allen COMPTON
Child #14 md(2) Lena (Lumbus) BORAH

SOURCES OF INFORMATION
11. TIB record for endowment dates and bapt. dates of children #11, 14.
12. Salt Lake Temple for sealing of children to parents.

© 1972 The Gene... ...ety of The Church of Jesus Christ of Latter-day Saints, Inc.
Deseret Book Company, Salt Lake City, Utah

About the Author

Following retirement from the Bureau of Reclamation in 1987, I published Grandpa Neibaur Was a Pioneer, a book about this great-great-great grandfather, Alexander Neibaur, who was the first Jew to join the Church of Jesus Christ of Latter-Day Saints, and was Utah's first dentist. His life and testimony fascinate me and I continually want to know more about him and his family. I keep coming back to his journal to gather inspiration for poetry.

I have written poetry all my life. In Star Valley High School in Afton, Wyoming, I won second place in an English poetry competition. After graduation, I became a long distance telephone operator in Ogden, Utah. There I met and married LaVell Butt, who was in the Navy. I worked as an operator in San Diego, CA and Salt Lake City.

My government career includes the VA Hospital, the U.S. Postal Service, and the Bureau of Reclamation. Three sons were born before my postal career, my daughter during that time. In the Public Affairs writing returned prominently to the foreground. I wrote news releases, speeches, and articles for the byline of the Bureau of Reclamation's Regional Director. The last four years I edited their monthly newsletter, The Spillway and The Colorado River Project Annual Report.

After retirement, I attended poetry classes at Pioneer Crafthouse. For three years I edited the USPS biannual Poetry Panorama, and I am still learning as I teach poetry classes at Pioneer Crafthouse. My love for writing does not diminish. I am currently president of the Utah State Poetry Society.

Other writing appears in Byline Magazine, Utah English Journal, 1995, The Sandcutters, California Quarterly, Prize Winning Poems 1995, Reclamation Era, Craft 'N Things, Golden Age, Utah Sings, Volumes IV, V, and VII, Poetic Page, Poetry Panorama, Zarahemla, The Unsung, Midge, and Neibaur Neighbor.

I live in Murray, Utah, close to my four married children and 16 grandchildren.